THEY DIED TOO YOUNG

JOHN LENNON

Tom Stockdale

CHELSEA HOUSE PUBLISHERS
Philadelphia

First published in traditional hardback edition
©1998, 2001 by Chelsea House Publishers, a subsidiary of
Haights Cross Communications.
Printed in Hong Kong
Copyright © Parragon Book Service Ltd 1995
Unit 13–17, Avonbridge Trading Estate, Atlantic Road
Avonmouth, Bristol, England BS11 9QD

Illustrations courtesy of Rex Features

Library of Congress Cataloging-in-Publication Data
Stockdale, Tom.
　　John Lennon / by Tom Stockdale.
　　　　p.　　cm. — (They died too young)
　　Originally published: Avonmounth, Bristol : Parragon,
1995.
　　Summary: Presents the life of John Lennon, from his early
years through the rise and breakup of the Beatles to his final
days in New York.
　　ISBN 0-7910-4633-8　(hc)
　　1. Lennon, John, 1940-　　—Juvenile literature. 2. Rock
musicians—England—Biography—Juvenile literature.
　[1. Lennon, John, 1940-　　2. Musicians. 3. Rock music.]
I. Title.
II. Series.
ML3930.L34S76　1997
782.42166'092—dc21
　[B]　　　　　　　　　　　　　　　　　　　　97-19849
　　　　　　　　　　　　　　　　　　　　　　　CIP
　　　　　　　　　　　　　　　　　　　　　　MN AC

CONTENTS

John performing with the Beatles on the British television show Ready, Steady, Go

EARLY YEARS

John Lennon was born during an air raid on October 9,
1940, in a Liverpool that trembled under the nightly
German attacks of the Battle of Britain. His life would be
one that blew its own winds of change into the growing
mass culture of the postwar world, a life that, by its innovation and controversy, will stand as an example of personal striving and musical excellence for much longer than
the forty years he lived.

John's mother, Julia, gave him the patriotic middle name
Winston (after Britain's wartime prime minister Winston
Churchill) and struggled to bring him up while her husband,
Freddie, was at sea with the merchant navy. By the time
Freddie returned in November 1944, Julia had met a Welsh
soldier and was pregnant by him, and had left baby John
with his uncle. The new baby was adopted, and Freddie
brought John back and tried to patch up the marriage.

However, the attractive Julia had fallen for another man, John Dykins, and moved in with him in 1946.

Hence John's early life was one of instability, and his character soon showed the results: he was thrown out of nursery school for misbehavior. His despairing father had gone back to sea, believing that there was no hope for a family life, and didn't know that John had been farmed out to Julia's sister, Mimi. Mimi, a model of propriety, lent stability to John's life, but her strictness was a source of contention for the aggressive child. He was forced into the confines of the middle-class culture that his aunt planned for him, though her husband, George, would sometimes manage to slip him in to see a Western at the local movie theater. His enforced loneliness made him the center of his own world, and the combination of aggression and ego helped to explain much of the trouble that his quick tongue caused later on.

At school he suffered from undiagnosed dyslexia, an affliction that was in some ways a gift, for it brought a quirky style to his literary work. His teachers were more concerned with his bad manners, stealing, and bullying of other pupils at Dovedale Primary School, where he was at the head of an unruly gang of boys. By the time he moved on to Quarry Bank Grammar School in September 1952 his neighborhood knew who the likely culprit was if a firework went off in their mailbox, or if their daughters came home crying from school.

From about this time John recovered his relationship with his mother, whom he found a fun-loving alternative to the dictatorial Mimi. The brooding anger of *Rebel Without a Cause* and the explosion of rock 'n' roll that Bill Haley brought to Britain in 1955 was perfect for the rebellious youth. Julia's home was a base from which he was allowed more freedom, especially after the death of Mimi's husband, George. Julia was accepting of John's first serious girlfriend, and bought him his first guitar after the effect of Elvis

They Died Too Young

Presley's "Heartbreak Hotel" gave him the musical itch. Britain was rocking to the touring bands from America, like Fats Domino, Eddie Cochran, and, one of Lennon's big influences, Little Richard.

The sixteen-year-old Lennon formed his own band in 1957, the Quarrymen (named after Quarry Bank School, which most of the band attended). The Quarrymen played a gig on July 6, 1957, where Lennon was introduced to James Paul McCartney. Although he was a year younger than John, Paul was a better guitar player and impressed Lennon with a rendition of Eddie Cochran's "Twenty Flight Rock" to get himself a place in the band. Paul wanted a friend of his, George Harrison, to join the Quarrymen but Harrison was only fourteen. Although he proved his guitar skills, Lennon would not let him join for a year.

The Quarrymen were together until 1959, when they imploded in arguments and a final fight, giving them no chance of emulating the likes of Cliff Richard at the top of the charts. By this time Mimi had managed to get John into Liverpool College of Art, even though his test scores were poor. His new style was the thin, black-clothed look of the beatnik, which stood out among the more conservatively dressed students. He carried his disruptive tactics from the classroom into the art studio. Meanwhile, McCartney and Harrison were studying at the Liverpool Institute next door, and the three would play and sing through lunch and break times. John and Paul agreed early on that they would be credited as a partnership on any songs that they wrote, together or separately.

Lennon's behavior became even less stable after the death of his mother in 1958. She was run over by an off-duty policeman who was driving without a license, and who received only a reprimand and suspension as a punishment. John's bullying became more violent, and he would often pick fights. His hurtfulness and cynicism seemed to be the only defense he had against the vulnerability he felt.

John with his first wife, Cynthia

Lennon had started going steady with Cynthia Powell, a fellow art student. Her parents were very much against their relationship, but Cynthia believed she could bring out his gentle side. By this time, assured of failing his exams, he had moved into the apartment of his friend Stuart Sutcliffe, to form a new band around himself, Paul, and George. Sutcliffe, a talented art student, gave up his studies when offered the bass player's job, and it was he who came up with a name for the band, after the motorcycle gang from the film *The Wild One,* the Beetles. The name also alluded to Buddy Holly's Crickets, and was given a rhythmic slant by Lennon, turning the "beet" into "beat" and the Beetles into The Beatles.

The Cavern Club (seen today), one of The Beatles early gigs

WHAT THE WORLD WAS WAITING FOR

By 1960 Britain was full of Elvis clones, with Cliff Richard at their head, and the softer rock of Roy Orbison and Ritchie Valens was coming over from America. As a port city, Liverpool was more accessible than some of Britain's inland locations and so had the advantage of hosting a wider range of American imports. The Liverpool scene was one of cheap dance nights and running gang battles, and The Silver Beatles, as they were called for a while, found it hard to get a gig behind tough rock 'n' roll outfits like Cass and the Casanovas. However, a good performance in the presence of talent scout Larry Parnes got them a short tour of Scotland backing one of Parnes's finds, Johnny Gentle. The Beatles' drummer, Tommy Moore, pulled out of the band after the tour, so the rest of the band tried to persuade Pete Best to leave his band, The Blackjacks. He was won over by The Beatles' chance to go to Hamburg, Germany. Allan Williams, owner of a club and coffee bar, had already sent a few bands to play in some of the clubs there, and in August 1960 he got The Beatles a booking at the Club Indra.

It took only one performance in front of the drunken crowds of the Hamburg club for the band to realize that just standing and singing was not going to go down well. They quickly learned how to draw an audience with onstage antics and rowdy behavior that they kept up during draining seven-hour sets. Soon the band was receiving crates of beer, thrown onto the stage, and were often as drunk as the audience. They returned to Hamburg in the spring of 1961, playing at the Top Ten Club, where the party continued. Stuart Sutcliffe fell in love with a German woman, Astrid Kircherr, and soon left the band to be with her and to return to his art.

Back in Liverpool, with the advantage of their experience in Germany, The Beatles found it easy to get gigs in the low-ceilinged basement of a warehouse called the Cavern Club. With an exciting show and wealth of material they were soon a popular attraction, and a version of "My Bonnie" that they recorded with singer Tony Sheridan was in demand at the NEMS record shop, run by Brian Epstein. Intrigued by a single that was outselling established bands, he made what would be the first of many visits to the Cavern in October 1961, and became infatuated by the band. In January 1962 he became their manager, although he would be learning this new trade as he went along. By then The Beatles had been voted top group by Liverpool's *Mersey Beat* magazine.

In April 1962 The Beatles were headlining at Hamburg's Star Club, though they were met at the airport with the shocking news that Stuart Sutcliffe had died of a brain hemorrhage that resulted from a fight some months previously. The Star Club bookings were to prove the making of The Beatles, although John's behavior worsened with Sutcliffe's death.

On January 1 the band had made a demo for Decca that was rejected. The tape found its way to George Martin at EMI, who gave them a session in June. Martin was dissatisfied with the drumming of Pete Best, so Best was replaced with the plainer face but more stable beat of Richard Starkey, known as Ringo Starr. Martin was wary of allowing the band to do their own material, but a McCartney song,

"Love Me Do," became their first single. Of the second, Lennon's composition "Please Please Me," Martin declared, "Gentlemen, you've just made your first number one record."

In between the recording of "Please Please Me" and the confirmation of George Martin's prophecy in February 1963, Lennon married Cynthia on August 23, and the band recorded an album during one night in the middle of a nationwide tour. From the opening notes of "I Saw Her Standing There" to the closing chords of "Twist and Shout," The Beatles laid down a fresh, raw, and very English adaptation of the American rock that grabbed their audiences, giving them the headlining role on a tour in March, and beginning a songwriting roller coaster that turned the world upside down.

John, Paul, George, and Ringo making history in an early performance

BEATLEMANIA

On April 8, 1963, Cynthia Lennon gave birth to a son, John Charles Julian Lennon. The child did not meet his father for a week, and this lack of contact became the pattern in Julian Lennon's life. John was in the first flush of stardom; not only was he very busy but he was also inclined to ignore the mundane responsibilities of family life. He hid his marriage from the world for eighteen months, during which time his lifestyle was very much that of a bachelor. He continued to suffer fits of drunken violence, and his change of character under various influences was something for his closest friends to be wary of.

The instant influence of The Beatles is obvious from the album charts of 1963. *Please Please Me* took the number one spot from Cliff Richard's *Summer Holiday* in May and relinquished it only to *With The Beatles* in December, as part of a full year at the top. In fact, only the Rolling Stones, Bob Dylan, and *The Sound of Music* would dislodge the band from their perch until February 1967. The singles charts would allow a glimpse of acts following in the wake of The Beatles, such as the Animals, the Kinks, the Hollies, and The Spencer Davis Group.

"Beatlemania" was the term coined to describe the reactions of the screaming youngsters who lost control every time The Beatles were mentioned. The band's appearance on the 1963 *Royal Variety Show* in Britain sealed the approval of the nation, complete with Lennon's cheeky dig at the audience: "The people in the cheap seats clap your hands. All the rest of you, if you'll just rattle your jewelry." It was the sort of comment that made press interviews with The Beatles a joy for everyone. They were led in this by John, whose humor and intelligence made him good copy on any subject, and he had some effect in changing people's previous attitude that rock music was simply a last chance for high school dropouts.

The leap of "I Want to Hold Your Hand" to number one in America was a unique event for a group that had not set foot in the country, and in February 1964 the band left to claim their crown. The scenes at the airports, on *The Ed Sullivan Show,* and at the concerts completed their musical takeover, with viewing figures of almost seventy-four million for the television appearance, and gigs at which the screaming was louder than the music. By April they held the top five positions in the American singles chart.

They followed their triumph with *A Hard Day's Night,* a film that may have been planned merely as a vehicle for the soundtrack but was successful in its own right. The album also gained an audience beyond that of the screaming teens, since the Lennon–McCartney partnership showed a depth way beyond the usually crass songwriting efforts of teen idols. Their musical collage fashioned something totally new out of just about every influential sound flying through the ether. "The greatest composers since Beethoven," declared the London *Sunday Times.* From then on, self-penned compositions would become the norm for artists who had formerly been a showcase for the talents of others.

Later in 1964 the band undertook a world tour that repeated endlessly the format of ecstatic crowds, constant police protection, and wild parties that belied the impression of their public image. In between their three hits of the year they left just a little room for songs by others to get to the top of the singles charts. Lennon became a best-selling author with his books *John Lennon in His Own Write* and *A Spaniard*

Yoko and John with John's son Julian Lennon

Lennon signing autographs in Paris

in the Works, and the band released *Beatles for Sale.* By 1965 The Beatles could do no wrong, and Lennon found that uncouth public displays just bounced off the image that had been manufactured for him. "Help" and "Nowhere Man" display his attempts to describe in song the pressures he was feeling, and the albums *Rubber Soul* and *Revolver* witnessed his efforts to define himself with lyrics that left behind the straightforward love songs of the earlier albums. He had bought a mock-Tudor mansion near Weybridge, England, but used very few of its many rooms. After the rigors of touring that had continued until September 1965, he almost hibernated there, getting stoned and playing with expensive toys and cars. His relationship with Cynthia and Julian was minimal, and he apparently felt an emptiness that could not be filled by his family. Lennon had tried LSD several times before, but now attempted a serious examination of its powers. His ironic sense of humor and his natural tendency to speak his mind were an explosive mixture to add to the self-knowledge that LSD claims for its users.

By 1966 The Beatles had already received death threats in Japan, and a physical beating as they left the Philippines after Epstein had turned down an audience with Imelda Marcos. They received more threats during their dates in the southern United States, and by the end of the tour had decided never to do another. Lennon went straight into the filming of Richard Lester's film *How I Won the War* in Germany and Spain, leaving Britain to the hit song of another Liverpool son, Ken Dodd and "Tears." John returned to continue his LSD journey in London, where, on November 9, 1966, he met artist Yoko Ono at an avant-garde exhibition at the Indica Gallery. Ono had rejected the possibilities open to her as a member of a wealthy Japanese family, choosing to live the creative life in New York. Her artistic credibility was not high among its prominent movers; but like the master of the scene, Andy Warhol, she could seize the opportunity when it arose, and, like Lennon, she was adept at making the most of a lucky set of influences. She was in London visiting a series of exhibitions with her husband, Tony Cox, and daughter, Kyoko, but she decided that Lennon was for her, and John was soon infatuated. Although there are differing accounts of their life together, it seems that they were inseparable within a short time of their meeting.

In 1967 the flower power movement was in full swing. It was the year of Procol Harem's "A Whiter Shade of Pale" and Scott McKenzie's "San Francisco," and The Beatles' album of that year, *Sgt. Pepper's Lonely Hearts Club Band,* became the monument of the era. Its technology and formulation gave it a unique place in the history of rock music, thanks to George Martin, but by now the driving force of The Beatles was Paul McCartney. John Lennon had never had the patience for drawn-out recording sessions, and Paul was much better able to handle the complications that six months of recording entailed. John did not just sit back, though; he was responsible for "Strawberry Fields Forever," "Lucy in the Sky with Diamonds" and the single at the center of the Sgt. Pepper experience, "All You Need Is Love." His resentment of Paul's dominance was a feature of a general frustration within the band, but it was probably McCartney's lead that kept them together at the time.

With George Harrison's encouragement, the band came under the influence of the Maharishi Mahesh Yogi and his antimaterialist teaching, and John was very taken with its promise of inner fulfillment. On August 27, 1967, they were in the middle of a five-day course with him when word came of Brian Epstein's death, apparently by suicide. Since The Beatles had become studio-based they needed less of his time, and his other businesses were not going well, although he had cut himself in for a good percentage of his main band. Distraught over the loss of another influential person in his life, Lennon turned to Yoko Ono for support.

The other main project of 1967 was *Magical Mystery Tour,* which contained Lennon's "I Am the Walrus," an overt

They Died Too Young

A tableau inspired by the Sgt. Pepper's *classic "All You Need Is Love"*

reference to Lewis Carroll (author of *Alice in Wonderland*) and a prime example of John's writing through a filtering of everyday experience. The film would premiere on television late in the year, and was the first Beatles product to be less than critically acclaimed. During its making John was reconciled with his father, Freddie. The two had met several times since 1964, but John had been unable to forgive Freddie for abandoning the family, until John's uncle explained to him about his parents' marital complications. John bought a house in Brighton for Freddie and his new bride, Pauline, and their meetings were, for the most part, friendly.

John and Cynthia were living almost separate lives by now, but they traveled together on a Beatles trip to the Maharishi's place of retreat in India in February 1968. The holy man's dubious morals were exposed during their stay and the party escaped immediately, canceling the guru's plans to star with the band on an American television show. Although the sojourn had produced a new group of songs, Lennon was cured of this particular spirituality.

He sank back into drug taking, sending the family off to Greece and secluding himself with his childhood friend Pete Shotton. By the time Cynthia returned John had decided to make his relationship with Yoko public, beginning with a symbolic acorn-planting at the National Sculpture Exhibition at Coventry Cathedral in central England in June 1968. This gave the press a cynical advantage for reports about the woman who had stolen the Beatle. They spent a "honeymoon" period at Ringo's apartment, which had once been occupied (and wrecked) by Jimi Hendrix. John and Yoko spent nearly a month at the apartment, living on champagne and caviar. They emerged for a Lennon art exhibition that displayed obvious Ono influences. When Yoko became pregnant in September 1968, Cynthia was given the upper hand in the ongoing divorce case, and by November she had a settlement and a trust fund for Julian, but Yoko's husband got a much better deal in his divorce.

Taking over from *The Hollies' Greatest Hits,* The Beatles album of 1968 was simply called *The Beatles* but is always known as the "White Album." Featuring many of the songs that had been written in India, it was a bag of individual numbers brought out under the band name, and remains an eclectic and impressive work, though it indicates the fragmentation of the band. The single "Hey Jude/Revolution" was the first release on Apple Records, the recording arm of Apple Corps, the company that the band formed to control their business affairs and through which they attempted to develop new artists like James Taylor and Mary Hopkin. At the same time John and Yoko brought out the album *Two Virgins.* The cover picture of the naked couple caused much more comment than its contents, an avant-garde collection of noises and sounds that was banned in America. The release was followed on October 18 by John and Yoko's arrest for drug possession.

Despite a rapid cleanup after a tip-off, small amounts of various drugs were discovered in the thorough search made by the police. Two weeks later Yoko suffered a miscarriage. A week after that they found themselves in court, where Lennon pleaded guilty for fear that Yoko would be deported if they fought the case. He received a fine and a threat of imprisonment if he was caught again. He had managed to crack the image he had been chipping away at for so long, but dispelling one myth didn't fill the emptiness he so often seemed to feel at his core.

John and Yoko made their relationship public in 1968

JOHN AND YOKO MOVE ON

At the beginning of 1969 The Beatles began work on *Let It Be*, which would end up being released after *Abbey Road*. Disruption was caused by an attempt to film them at work as part of their commitment to another movie project, and also by the presence of Yoko, who, unlike the partners of the other Beatles, insisted on being present in the studio. John tried to insist on a record free of studio technology, wanting a revivalist sound to accompany some of the early numbers they were again addressing, but it was asking the impossible of a group who no longer had the tightness that comes from regular live shows. In a final fit, they took the equipment to the flat roof of the studio and played a memorable live set, to the delight of the crowd that gathered in the street below.

The differences between the band members dissolved into hostility over the question of management. Paul put forward his future father-in-law, music-business lawyer Lee Eastman, as a candidate, but John preferred the choice of Allen Klein, accountant and Rolling Stones' manager. George and Ringo sided with John, and a disagreement during a meeting with the two hopefuls caused the McCartney block to walk out, in the start of a feud. Paul agreed eventually to have Klein investigate their financial situation, which was shown to be dire.

Brian Epstein's work in launching and presenting The

Beatles had been vital, but in almost every area of business he had sold them short, from the original record and publishing deals, to tax, touring, and merchandising. The band was able to access a tiny percentage of its worth, and much of what it had lost was gone forever. What must have been especially hard to accept was the loss of the rights to about two hundred songs to Sir Lew Grade's ATV company. The emotional loss must have been hard enough, and the songs' possible financial worth was borne out by their purchase by Michael Jackson in 1986 for $47.5 million. As a result of his work, Klein got the management deal with The Beatles on a three-to-one vote and successfully renegotiated several areas, most importantly the poor royalty rate.

While the business affairs were coming to light during March 1969, John and Yoko got married on a whim, going to Gibraltar for an instant ceremony. They followed the event with the first of the "bed-ins" (a variation on the sit-in style of protest popular at the time) at the Amsterdam Hilton, in a public advertisement for peace. John took to the new cause as energetically as he had his other attempts toward personal growth, and he was rewarded with worldwide coverage of his promotion, with its "Give peace a chance" banner. The media treatment made them popular with the antiwar groups, who considered the pair a welcome diversion from the less positive press they had been receiving of late. John and Yoko followed this with a "bag stunt" in Vienna, where they appeared before the press inside a closed-up bed cover, to make a statement against prejudice through visual stereotyping.

Their new identity as artists of controversy and promotion was described in Lennon's song from the time, "The Ballad of John and Yoko," and they proceeded to Toronto in May for another bed-in and the recording of "Give Peace a Chance" with a group of celebrities and fans in their hotel bedroom. By then John had taken the name "Ono" as a marital gesture to Yoko, who disliked the chauvinism of being

They Died Too Young

"Mrs. Lennon." It was also an opportunity for John to drop the patriotic "Winston," although he could not officially lose it without legal procedures.

The pressing need to work on *Abbey Road* caused the Lennons to return to England. They preceded it with a trip to Scotland with Julian and Kyoko, where John had spent the happiest times of his youth at his aunt's sheep farm. Thanks to John's erratic driving he crashed the car, causing facial injuries to himself and Yoko, and they were fixed up at the local hospital. The guilty white Austin Maxi was brought back to the new home, Tittenhurst Park, outside Sunningdale, England, and displayed on a concrete plinth in front of the living room as a memorial to a narrow escape. Another consequence of the accident was the placement of a large bed in the recording studio, where Yoko continued her recuperation while being able to monitor John's work. The result, released in September 1969 and displacing Blind Faith's album from the top spot, was a polished, professional album containing Lennon's "Come Together," with which he was very happy, and the second side's cleverly joined medley of McCartney-influenced technology, which John disdained.

That same month John and Yoko flew to Toronto as the result of a last minute agreement to play at a rock 'n' roll revival show promising Little Richard, Gene Vincent, and Chuck Berry. John's agreement to appear saved the undersold gig from folding, and his arrival with Eric Clapton, bassist Klaus Voorman, and drummer Alan White marked the first showing of the Plastic Ono Band. Lennon was very proud of the success of the band, and used it as an impetus to announce to The Beatles that he was finished with them. He was persuaded to delay a public announcement, for the new financial footing that Klein had prepared was dependent upon the success of album sales, which could be put into jeopardy by an official split of the band.

In October Yoko was hit by another miscarriage. John was sure that drug use was responsible for the failure of

Yoko's pregnancies, and attempted to dry out during a boat trip around Greece. Their return was marked by the *Wedding Album,* a collection of souvenirs accompanying an album of screaming and a press interview, and by Lennon's return of his MBE (a title conferred by the monarchy in recognition of service to the British Empire) to Buckingham Palace "in protest against Britain's involvement in the Nigeria-Biafra thing, against our support of the American troops in Vietnam and against 'Cold Turkey' slipping down the charts." Apart from the "Cold Turkey" quip, Lennon's gesture was, for him, a serious one. With his veteran's knowledge of media tactics and effect, he knew it would get media attention as part of his "peace offensive." The song "Cold Turkey" was the searing result of John's attempt to cut himself off from heroin without treatment. It would take an introduction to methadone to have any lasting effect on his habit.

That Christmas, billboards appeared in sites in major cities around the world, declaring "War is over! If you want it. Happy Christmas from John and Yoko." A Plastic Ono supergroup including George Harrison, Eric Clapton, Billy Preston, and Keith Moon played a "Peace for Christmas" concert at the Lyceum in London. Announcing plans for a worldwide music and peace conference near Toronto for the following year, Lennon met with Canadian prime minister Pierre Trudeau, which confirmed his status as an international presence for his cause. "The peace thing isn't a gimmick," he said. "Other people make it a gimmick. Yoko and I are serious."

In January 1970 the Lennons flew to Alborg, a small town in Denmark, where Tony Cox was living with his new wife and Kyoko, to discuss the unsettled details of Kyoko's custody. John and Cynthia had come to an agreement with regard to Julian, and John was trying to spend time with his son. While they were away, an exhibition of John's lithographs in London was raided by the police, who confiscated half of the works on grounds of indecency. Naturally sales of

They Died Too Young

John Lennon performing during his solo years

his pictures increased as a result of the publicity, and a court case in April 1970 would decide in favor of the gallery. The Lennons returned from Denmark with their hair shorn— they had traded the hair for a pair of Muhammad Ali's boxing shorts, planning to auction them in the cause of peace. John also declared that all future proceeds from his songs would go toward world peace. The proposed Toronto festival collapsed in arguments over money and organization, while John created, recorded, and released "Instant Karma" in ten days. He sang the Phil Spector–produced song on *Top of the Pops* in February, but did not knock Edison Lighthouse's "Love Grows (Where My Rosemary Goes)" from the top.

Just before the May release of the album *Let It Be* provided a gap in the long chart-supremacy of Simon and Garfunkel's *Bridge over Troubled Water*, Paul McCartney announced his retirement from The Beatles. The shockwave went around the world, but John had mentally left the group long before; the formal disbandment merely allowed him to proceed in his new direction with strength from the fact that there was nothing to look back to. A development in his forward momentum was a willingness to confront the terrors of his childhood. Arthur Janov's primal scream therapy taught that, by focusing on disturbances in earlier life and literally screaming them away, the psychological wounds that affected adult life could be healed. It was a theory tailor-made for Lennon, and he leaped onto its possibilities in the same way that he had his drug and spiritual enthusiasms. He and Yoko underwent a four-month course at the Institute in California, and the results were offered up in the self-conscious honesty of songs on the John Lennon/Plastic Ono Band album of December 1970. The new decade witnessed a new John Lennon in the deeply personal "Mother" and the rejection of pressures of the past in "God." "It was the most important thing that happened to me," he said of primal therapy, "besides meeting Yoko and being born."

One ugly result of this experience was a showdown with

his father, when John berated him for his failures as a parent, and sent him from the house. They would not talk again until Freddie was on his deathbed, and John regretted that they had not made up properly. Another, more public, outburst occurred in a *Rolling Stone* interview covering two issues in January–February 1971, when Lennon derided The Beatles and the sixties, declaring that the world was still the same unfair place that it had been before: "Nothing happened except we all dressed up."

John and Yoko in Central Park, New York City

NEW YORK

The Lennons' preoccupations in 1971 lasted for several
years. First was the division of The Beatles. The animosity
between John and Paul grew during the year, and was
made public in press interviews. Paul seemed to be belittling
John's activities, and John hit back with ferocity. McCartney's
application to the courts for the resolution of The Beatles'
finances provoked the holding of any future royalties in a
fund from which the four were allowed to draw an
allowance. This arrangement continued until the matter was
finalized in 1975.

Second, there was family, with the continuing conflict
over custody of Kyoko, now age eight. Tony Cox had disap-
peared with the child and surfaced in Majorca. John and
Yoko flew there, and, on April 23, Allen Klein was contacted
with the news that they were being held by the police after
Cox reported Kyoko missing from a playground. Cox slipped
off the island, while Klein managed to get the Lennons freed
without charge. They heard that Cox was in New York, and
John was successful in obtaining a nine-month visa beginning in June to search for Kyoko. This marked John's introduction to the city that became the Liverpool of his last
decade, one in which he felt at ease as an artist, and not like
a "guy who won the pools [lottery]."

Third, there was art. A series of John's avant-garde films

was shown in Cannes and London during the year. In *Erection,* the construction of a building over eighteen months was filmed through still-photos of the work. In *Apotheosis,* a camera was attached to a helium balloon that rose into the clouds, becoming a long visual white-out. The climax for John and Yoko was her exhibition at the Everson Museum of Fine Art in New York. Entitled *This Is Not Here,* the hastily assembled project was set in a massive space and featured as its centerpiece the "Water Event," consisting of one hundred donations by artists and celebrities on a water theme. John's gift was a pink object inside a plastic bag labeled "Napoleon's Bladder." Unfortunately the exhibition was trashed by an invasion of fans who wanted to see John Lennon. "What was meant to be was meant to be," said Yoko.

Imagine, the best-known of Lennon's solo albums, was recorded in the studio that he had set up at Tittenhurst and at the Record Plant in New York during July, and was released in October. Its commercial sound was topped with the plaintive simplicity of the title track, and was a welcome relief to the fans who had been confused by the harshness of his recent work. The film *Imagine,* which followed the album, was an arty profile of John and Yoko, memorable for the beauty of the scenes shot at Tittenhurst that accompanied the title track.

By this time they had settled permanently in New York. John immersed himself in the downtown area around Greenwich Village, sometimes in the company of street performer David Peel (for whose album John would be producer) and, occasionally, Bob Dylan. Part of John's association with the area was an involvement with its left-wing radicals, led by Jerry Rubin. The Lennons appeared at a rally in support of jailed White Panther leader John Sinclair, and at other political demonstrations. John was thus brought to the attention of immigration officials, who ordered his deportation after the expiration of his visa in February 1972. The pretext was Lennon's 1968 drug conviction, but the fear was that he was involved in a proposed disruption of the 1972 Republican Convention, and the political statements of his June 1972 album, *Some Time in New York City,* did not ease the nerves of a troubled and suspicious administration. Lennon's four-year battle for a green card would include his being watched, followed, and phone-tapped by the FBI to a degree that did not equate with the reason given for his deportation. As a result Lennon would be unable to leave America until 1976 for fear that he would not be allowed back in. A plus for the public was a profile-raising benefit for handicapped children that he played at Madison Square Garden in August 1972.

As though he didn't have enough problems to deal with going into 1973, Lennon decided to drop the management services of Allen Klein, who brought out a lawsuit for unrepaid loans. For most of the year Lennon hibernated at home, which had become the Dakota Building on the West Side of Manhattan, and he started work on the album *Mind Games.* The pressures of life were weighing heavy on him, and the resulting strain on his seemingly impregnable relationship with Yoko snapped it in the autumn. He began an eighteen-month period known as the "Lost Weekend," leaving for Los Angeles with his secretary, May Pang, when Yoko kicked him out. Yoko condoned the eventual relationship between John and May Pang; she knew that he had never been without a partner, and considered that one who relied on her for a salary was an obvious preference to an independent woman. May Pang was a steady, non-drug-taking girl, but nevertheless she could put little restraint on what became a return to the wild days of John's youth. It might well have been a necessary exorcism for a man who had attempted in many ways to address the demons within him, but it was a trying time for many of the people with whom he came into contact. He was thrown out of the Troubadour Club after a drunken swearing match, and smashed up the Bel Air house that record producer Lou Adler had lent him, forcing his friends to tie him to a bed to stop the mayhem.

He had gathered a select group of musicians to record a rock 'n' roll covers album produced by Phil Spector, and the sessions dissolved into drunkenness and arguments between star and producer. *Mind Games* was released in the middle of the sessions, and its professional sound must have made Lennon even more frustrated by the lack of progress. A final disrupted session before Christmas was followed by Spector's disappearance with the master tapes.

Lennon moved into a house with Harry Nilsson, Klaus Voorman, Keith Moon, and Ringo Starr, just some of the friends with whom he had been bar-hopping all over the city. During May 1974 he worked on and produced Nilsson's *Pussy Cats,* and this responsibility forced him to slow the pace a little. His alcoholic haze did clear enough for him to produce *Walls and Bridges,* released in October 1974, a beautifully packaged album containing his first number one American single, "Whatever Gets You Through the Night." As he said of the album, "I'm almost amazed that I could get anything out. . . . It was the work of a semi-sick craftsman." By this time Lennon was returning toward a normal existence. Back in New York in an apartment on East 52nd Street, he saw quite a bit of Mick Jagger, for whom he had a lot of respect, and met up with Paul McCartney. As a result of a bet with Elton John over the chart position of "Whatever Gets You Through the Night" (Elton had said it would be number one), Lennon appeared with him at Elton's Madison Square Garden concert in November.

By then Lennon was in negotiations with music publisher Morris Levy over a copyright infringement of the Levy-owned Chuck Berry song "You Can't Catch Me" on "Come Together" from *Abbey Road.* John had regained the Phil Spector masters after six months of trying, and, although only three tracks were worth saving, it was agreed that an album based around them would be brought out by Levy's budget mail-order company. Lennon put down ten tracks in

The Dakota Building on New York's Upper West Side, where John and Yoko lived

just a few days to complete the album. The problem was that they would need a release from EMI to bring the album out. John's lawyer talked him out of the project, but Levy ignored the dangers and the illegal *Roots* was on sale from February 1975. The official version, *Rock and Roll,* was rush-released by EMI/Capitol, and Levy's distribution was choked by threats from the powerful major label.

Order was restored in 1975. In January The Beatles were officially divorced, and John got back together with Yoko, although she did not let him move in formally until March. He had certainly regained his optimism and he continued his creative form, working with David Bowie on his *Young Americans* album and cowriting Bowie's first American number one, "Fame." And finally, John and Yoko had been working to "clean up their act," and soon after their reconciliation Yoko became pregnant.

They had agreed, on John's return, that he should have some sort of life outside the Dakota Building, and he would spend time at Montauk, New York, on the Long Island coast. They had a symbolic second marriage, and agreed that he would take care of the child, allowing Yoko to take over the breadwinning role. John Lennon, held up as a symbol of success and innovation around the world, was determined to be a success at the one thing that had been at the root of so many problems in his life: family. His five-year retirement indicates the strength of his commitment to the ideal.

On October 9, 1975, John's thirty-fifth birthday and two days after a court's reversal of his deportation order, Yoko gave birth to a son by Caesarean section. The delivery was delicate, and John blew up at a doctor's request for an auto-graph as Yoko was coming out of sedation. The birth was treated by him as a miracle, and Sean Taro Ono Lennon was also treated as such. As a conclusion to the era, the compilation album *Shaved Fish,* released just after Sean's birth, was a compact résumé of John's recent music, and would be the last that fans would hear of him for five years.

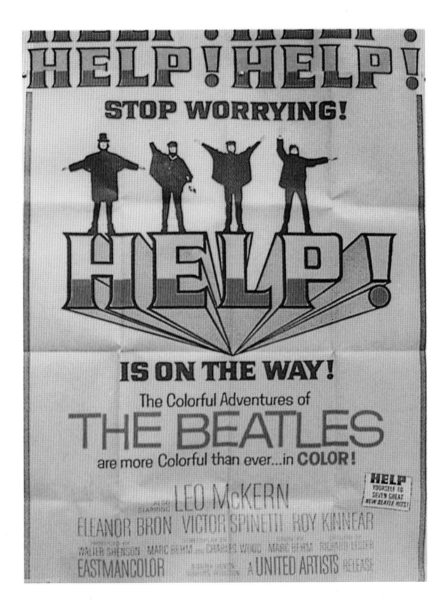

Rare one-sheet movie poster from the Beatle's second movie, Help!

*A tribute to John Lennon outside the Dakota building
in Manhattan, where he was shot*

TRAGEDY

For the next few years Yoko built up a portfolio of property, buying houses and farms, including a herd of dairy cows, one of which fetched a record $265,000 at auction. "Only Yoko Ono could sell a cow for a quarter of a million dollars," joked John. She bought up several of the apartments in the Dakota, and a retreat overlooking the Atlantic on Long Island, the only one of their many other residences that the Lennons used regularly. Her business techniques placed great emphasis on the use of astrology and numerology, not usually deemed important in the corporate world. The tarot cards also affected any travel plans; direction and time of journeys were vital to her, thus the family's yearly trip to Japan might involve them traveling separately and in different directions. Yoko's reliance on such practices made her vulnerable to less-than-scrupulous characters among psychic practitioners, and some of the artifacts that made their way into the Lennon houses were vastly overpriced "psychic necessities."

Lennon allowed Yoko's priorities to take the lead, as he immersed himself in his duties as a house-husband, proudly sending a photo of his first self-baked loaf of bread to his friend Elliot Mintz in California. His devotion to Sean gave him no patience for most of the worldly activities that had taken up his time in the past, and he swamped the boy with expensive toys in a plan of "overmaterialization," to give

Sean a disregard of such things. He was an unsuccessful student of Japanese, and took several unnoticed trips around the world—he would delight in his anonymity, until, of course, he handed over a credit card.

In the first half of 1976 John was stricken by the deaths of his father, one of his aunts, and the tragic killing of Beatles retainer Mal Evans, and he believed himself to be marked out for an early death. He managed to accommodate his continued weakness for drugs with a strict health regime that made him noticeably thin. But he finally grew closer to Julian, now aged thirteen, teaching him to play the guitar and spending time with him on vacation. John disliked most of the rock music of the late 1970s, and he took to listening to music from earlier in the century, especially Bing Crosby. For John's thirty-eighth birthday Yoko gave him a Wurlitzer that played only 78 rpm records.

In August 1980 Lennon's love of the sea was fulfilled by an ocean voyage from Rhode Island to Bermuda with a five-man crew. The rough seas that they encountered gave him a new sense of himself, and his safe arrival sparked off a fit of songwriting, news of which was flashed around the world. Yoko had also been writing again, and the couple agreed to share an album. John got some musicians together—for an occasion like this he could take his pick of the crop—and he recorded over twenty songs with a speed that impressed all around him. The publicity campaign was headed by an interview for *Playboy* magazine, and the label of release was to be the recently formed Geffen Records, because owner David Geffen was willing to take the record without hearing it.

Double Fantasy was released on November 17, 1980, a double album showcasing John's emotional stability in the lyrical maturity of "(Just Like) Starting Over" and "Woman," and the long-term influence of the 1950s in the treatment of his recorded voice. He had just celebrated his fortieth birthday, and was feeling ready to capitalize on his rediscovered muse with more writing. Though thin, and due to undergo

They Died Too Young

Yoko with Sean Lennon

an operation for the rebuilding of his drug-damaged nose, he was displaying an energy that no one could deny; and, despite only lukewarm critical reviews for the album, there was a general excitement about the prospect of his potential in the 1980s.

Everything was brought to a sudden and tragic stop at 10:50 P.M. on December 8. Twenty-five-year-old Mark Chapman, Lennon fan and born-again Christian who had gotten Lennon to autograph a copy of *Double Fantasy* earlier that day, put four bullets into John's back as he returned from the studio. John died at Roosevelt Hospital, within a short time of being rushed there by the first policemen to arrive at the scene. The world mourned, and Yoko retreated for several days in the Dakota, where a quarter of a million letters of sympathy would arrive during the next two months.

The shock of the killing had an immediate effect on a whole generation, which realized what Lennon had meant to it. The obvious result of his death would be the number one chart position for Lennon material, new and old. The symbol of John Lennon's influence was the ten minutes' silence joined by millions around the world, led by over a hundred thousand people in Central Park, on December 14, 1980, four days after his cremation at Hartsdale Crematorium, New York. They were all acknowledging the inspiration of a man who put his unique life and search for growth into a form that has affected popular music to this day. We cannot even guess at what he might have achieved if he had been allowed to live a full life.

John in the early days with The Beatles

INDEX

INDEX

John Lennon's Rolls Royce